I0830252

OTHER BOOKS AUTHORED BY DR OLERIBE INCLUDE

- Repositioning for Marital Success
- Celebrating Marital Success
- Making Maximum Impact in Life – The Keys
- Scaling New Heights
- Vital Leadership Thoughts and Nuggets
- The Concept of Child Abuse
- Fundamentals of Child Rights
- ADJS at 40: Celebrating Excellence, Consolidating the Vision (Editor)

TRANSFORMING IDEAS FOR ENTREPRENEURSHIP AND GREATNESS

OBINNA OSITADIMMA OLERIBE

authorHOUSE

AuthorHouse™
1663 Liberty Drive
Bloomington, IN 47403
www.authorhouse.com
Phone: 1 (800) 839-8640

Published by AuthorHouse 11/21/2019

ISBN: 978-1-7283-3685-5 (sc)
ISBN: 978-1-7283-3683-1 (hc)
ISBN: 978-1-7283-3684-8 (e)

Library of Congress Control Number: 2019919857

Print information available on the last page.

Dedication

Dedicated to my Daughter Delight Chimziterem, an amazing young woman full of ideas and plans

And to all

My sons and daughters across the nations of the world whose processed and implemented ideas will soon change the entire world

Contents

Acknowledgment

I thank God for the gift of life and health, and the ability to put this book together.

I want to thank all staff of Excellence and Friends Management Care Centre (EFMC) Abuja (2016 – 2018) who listened to me over several Monday prayers as I developed this idea and processed it. Particularly, I want to thank Grace Iyalla, Temitope Ishola, and Shola Oke who transcribed my messages into blogs that has today formed the basis of this book.

I sincerely appreciate Chisom O Anukam, MaryJane C Anike and Margret M Odiegwu for reading and editing the original manuscript.

Finally, I want to appreciate my wife, Princess Osita-Oleribe who together, we developed and piloted these ideas from the seasons of poverty to where we are today.

God bless you all.

Preface

*Life is all about ideas. Everyone has one. Only
a few benefit from ideas as only processed
and implemented ideas make great.*

Microsoft, Amazon, Boeing, Apple, Nokia, Rolex, etc. were once mere ideas in somebody's head. But today, they have not only changed the world, but have also brought to the owners humongous wealth. Every house, cloth, watch, shoe, business enterprise, establishment, etc. are all products of ideas.

Ideas rule the world. And anyone and everyone have ideas. But not everyone is ruling – why? This is because only processed and implemented ideas are profitable and beneficial to the initiator.

Of millions of ideas generated daily, only a little percentage see the light of day, and a smaller number is processed to products and profits.

In this life manual, I have condensed most of the things you need to know about ideas into a few pages. The book starts with the essence of ideas, the metamorphosis of ideas, people in the idea world, sources of idea, idea processes and purpose, to idea implementation and implementation cycle.

There are also segments on idea protection and turning ideas into projects. This discussion on ideas heralds the entrepreneur's segments with effective discussions on the IP4 of entrepreneurship, how to become a successful entrepreneur and the entrepreneurial process.

This short book is what you need to turn your golden ideas (by the way, all ideas, when processed, are golden) into products and profits. Let's take a walk together as we learn what to do with the ideas in your head right now.

Chapter 1: KEY ESSENCE OF IDEAS

Why ideas? What is the essence of ideas? Why is it so important to talk about ideas? The primary essence of idea is to solve problems. Ideas are programmed to solve life and human problems. However, that is not why men process and implement ideas. Men process and implement ideas primarily for profiting. People can profit from an idea as individuals, families, or organizations. Ideas allow us to profit in the works of our hands and in our careers.

The essence of ideas is for profiting. Any idea that does not end in profit is not worth pursuing. Ideas can profit us in various dimensions - financial, marital, career, and/ or intellectual profits. For any idea to stand the test of time, it must be an idea that delivers profit.

When the weave-on women wear was designed, it was not just designed to make women look and appear beautiful, but primarily to solve a problem and in solving that problem, make profits. Imagine the amount of money people who make weave-on and other hair products make every year from just this idea – especially among the black population? The clothes, shoes, phones, and everything around you are people's ideas designed to solve identified problems. But the initiator of these ideas developed them primarily to make profit.

If the idea will not deliver profit, it will not last long. There is, therefore, no need to just run with every idea. You must take a second look at the idea and check if the idea will be profitable.

<u>The Marketing Mix of Ideas:</u>

To achieve this, let us look at the marketing mix of ideas. In Economics, we have the expanded marketing mix of Product, People, Place, Price, Promotion, Production and Packaging. This is the 7Ps of ideas.

The Product: Every idea must be linked to a product, either a currently existing product or a product to be developed to solve a need/problem. Every idea that will be profitable must be linked to a product as people will not purchase ideas, but products.

Idea generated products could be tangible products or intangible products. Examples of intangible products (also called services) are communication services, healthcare services, training, etc; while tangible products include drugs, phones, houses, etc. Every profitable idea must be transformed into a product. Before you begin to run with any idea, always ask questions as to what product the idea is linked to. Is it a tangible product or an intangible product? This is critical as no idea can yield profits without a product. Clearly define the products your idea is linked to and or the new products it must create.

The People: Ideas that are profitable must be linked to people. There are two kinds of problems – natural and man-made problems. Useful ideas solve these problems. Ideas that solve man recognized problems are profitable to the initiator. Thus, profitable ideas must respond to problems that men have – they must serve people. An idea may serve an animal, but the animal must serve people;

or it may solve structural problems, but the structures belong to people. This is key as your profitability is hidden in three factors: people, problem and opportunities.

So, if your idea must bear fruit and be profitable, it must serve people. It usually does not serve all the people as it conventionally serves a particular segment of the people: food-related ideas for those who are hungry, accommodation ideas for the homeless, car servicing ideas for car owners, healthcare ideas for the sick, educational ideas for the ignorant or those who desire to go to school, etc. Ideas, therefore, are programmed to serve a well-defined segment of the population. If your ideas cannot meet people's needs, then profit is farfetched. Why? The money you are looking for are in people's pockets. Do a simple market segmentation and define the ideal population for your idea.

The Place: Every profitable idea is linked to a place for its development, implementation and marketing. For instance, there are ideas that will work well in the USA, but may not work well in Nigeria. While others may work very well in Nigeria and yield so much profit to you, but may not be very successful in the USA. There are ideas for urban, rural, cities, metropolitan, developed, developing, war ravaged, etc. areas of the world.

It is important to understand that every idea has a particular place for it to be developed, implemented and maintained. For someone looking for a place to buy a land, it is easier to buy land in Abuja Nigeria than in South East. Building an industry may be better where the raw materials are found. Establishing a club or eatery may be more successful in cities and towns where people are in a hurry or love night life, than in villages and rural areas. Basic educational institutions should be established in places where those who have infants and under-fives live or marketed to those who can afford them irrespective of where they live.

Every idea is linked to a place. Identify the ideal place for your idea.

The Price: For any idea to be profitable, there is a price to pay. Every idea has a two-directional price to pay. There is a price to pay before the idea is transformed into a functional product (by the idea initiator); there is also a price to pay to access and use the product(s) of the idea (by the users and customers). Unwillingness to pay the right price may deny us access to the profits in the ideas.

Highly profitable ideas are not cheap. Cheap ideas will deliver cheap profits. You want an idea that will make a difference in the world? They are expensive - they will cost you energy, intellectual prowess, time and money. In every idea, there are people to it, there are people that will use the idea products, and there are people that will work with you to see the idea comes to light.

The Packaging: For an idea to be profitable, it must be well packaged. It may not be born well packaged, but it is your responsibility to repackage it to be acceptable and attractive to the people who will use or fund it. In every aspect, packaging is fundamental. For instance, if you want to get a job this year, you must package your Curriculum Vitae. Your appearance can make someone like or hate you. If you want to buy clothes or food, you normally look at their packaging.

How you package your ideas and idea generated products determines how far they will go. There may be no profit if they are not well packaged. You should package your thoughts, your ideas, your processes, your products and even your marketing events to attract patronage and buy-ins. Define your packaging objectives and identify your packaging cost. Good packaging is expensive. Plan for it.

The Promotion: No matter how good your ideas, products and packaging are, if there are no promotions, your idea may never succeed. You may have the best products, the best packages, the best solutions to people's problems, but if you do not promote them, people will never buy them.

What people are ignorant about, they will not invest in. Why do you think Coca-Cola spend millions of dollars every year on products promotion? People need to know about you and see you on regular basis before they will add you to their budget. If your target population do not know about your products and services, they may never be able to invest in them. What you do not promote dies. For your idea to succeed, it must be promoted in season and out of season. Budget and plan your promotion activities now.

The Production: For your idea to succeed, there must be adequate preparation and provision to enhance the production of the products or services. You must be willing to produce adequate amount of its products to be able to achieve the needs of the people – supply must be in tandem with demand, and people must have unhindered access to sustain demands and improve profits.

This is because; there is power in number as a $1 profit in 1,000,000 products is better than a $100 profit in 100 products. Number is very empowering, and this depends on production capacity of the company for the idea. You must make plans to produce at the right rate, quality and quantity to meet the needs and demands of the people whose problems are solved by your idea. Make adequate plans.

For an idea to be profitable, always think about the 7Ps of marketing: The P of product, the P of people, the P of place, the P of price, the P of promotion, the P of packaging and the P of production.

Interlude 1: Nature of Ideas

Anyone can have an idea, only the pursued and implemented idea becomes **The Idea**. *Obinna Oleribe*

The wise only possess ideas; the greater part of mankind is possessed by them. *Samuel Taylor Coleridge*

The value of an idea has nothing whatsoever to do with the sincerity of the man who expressed it. *Oscar Wilde*

Daring ideas are like chessmen moved forward; they may be beaten, but they may start a winning game. *Johann Wolfgang Von Goethe*

An idea that is not dangerous is unworthy of being called an idea at all. *Elbert Hubbard*

An idea to be suggestive must come to the individual with the force of a revelation. *William James*

Unprocessed idea is a useless and avoidable burden to the bearer. *Obinna Oleribe*

Chapter 2: METAMORPHOSIS OF IDEAS

Ideas are imaginations, images, and or concepts that run through our minds. Everybody has ideas. But not everybody profits from ideas. Anybody can generate ideas either from personal, environmental, circumstances, experiences etc., but not everybody benefits from these ideas. Why?

To be profitable, every idea must go through a cycle of metamorphosis or they may never yield good results. It requires you taking the unformed amorphous idea into its metamorphosis cycle for you to benefit maximally from the ideas.

Phases of idea metamorphosis

1. **The raw idea.** This is the idea that you just conceived or generated. You may have ideas relating to your business, career, education, finances, marriage, etc. If it ends at this level of idea, you may be frustrated. There are many frustrated ideas that have never been beneficial to the individual. If an idea is not transformed from this raw state to the next level, the individual will be frustrated.

2. **Visions:** An idea may metamorphose into *visions*. Most visions began as mere ideas. All visions are products of ideas and usually represent the

bigger picture of an idea. Visions are ideas that have evolved up to a point where they can hold and or engage the individual. Visions are not just anything, but they are ideas that have moved from mere concepts to becoming an engaging concept that give people a reason for living. Most visions are products of *"revelational"* ideas – i.e. ideas from a superior realm.

3. **Missions:** Ideas can also metamorphose from an unformed concept through visions into a ***mission***. A mission is the driving force of visions. *Missions are visions on the go*. Every idea becomes fruitful when they are transformed into visions and then missions. Without a mission, your idea may even bring you pain and life will be full of misery. It is mission that erodes miseries in life.

4. **Projects:** Ideas can then be transformed from mere ideas into ***projects***. It is only when ideas become projects that they become profitable to the individual. Ideas easily become projects because every idea generated has a root problem it is designed to solve and when an idea is transformed into a project, it becomes profitable.

Every idea can be transferred and is time sensitive. If you do not run with an idea as quickly as is necessary, someone else will run with it. Ideas do not wait for you.

As quickly as you get the ideas, you are expected to begin to run with them and in running with them you turn your idea into a **vision** (if it is *revelational*), a **mission** that will drive you, and into a **project** that will guarantee your profit. Until your idea becomes a project, they will not yield income. Many people have awesome ideas that have remained at the level of ideas and that way, there are no benefits from them.

In summary, ideas can metamorphose into Vision, Mission, Projects, and Profits. To have ideas is not a big deal, what you do with them will determine if an idea will be beneficial to you or not. Has that idea been able to metamorphose into a vision, a mission, and/or a project?

The process of transforming your ideas into visions, missions, and projects takes time, skills and several other resources. This is why you must learn to guard your ideas as there are things that could hinder your ideas from changing from mere ideas to a project.

Interlude 2: Essence of idea

Ideas rule the world. *Unknown*

Ideas in creative hands and minds deliver an ideal world. *Obinna Oleribe*

Neither man nor nation can exist without a sublime idea. *Fyodor Dostoyevsky*

Ideas are a capital that bears interest only in the hands of talent. *Antoine De Rivarol*

Without ideas, the world is an endless wilderness and a deadly desert. *Obinna Oleribe*

Chapter 3: PEOPLE IN IDEAS

There are two major kinds of people in idea management – Negative Influencers (idea hinderers) and Positive Influencers (idea facilitators).

Negative Influencers

> ***Genesis 37:5 (KJV) And Joseph dreamed
> a dream, and he told it his brethren:
> and they hated him yet the more.***

This dream was an idea.

Beware of who you share your idea(s) with as there are all manner of people who may negatively affect your ideas. Negative Influencers (NI) include;

1. ***Idea killers:*** These are individuals whose major assignment is to kill good ideas. They are experts in discouraging people from taking steps while highlighting everything that may go wrong, will not work on possible risks and their cost implications. They use everything – age, sex, politics, environment, education, tribe, etc. to frighten people from pursuing their ideas. They see everything that will go wrong and never anything that may go well. They work hard to stop you from taking another step in line with the idea.

Beware of idea killers because they are everywhere. They may not be trying to kill it because they hate you, but may be working hard to kill the idea as the idea may put you ahead of them and this is one thing they do not want to happen. They may also be killing the idea because of past experiences or because they do not have the courage you have.

2. ***Idea stealers***: Some people are not killers of ideas, but mere stealers of ideas. These are individuals you share your ideas with and who afterwards go behind you to implement the ideas. They may even try to discourage you from implementing the ideas, while looking at how best they can appropriate the ideas to themselves. Idea stealers may discourage you from pursuing your ideas while working hard to implement the same idea either as it is or with little modification.

3. ***Idea abortionists***: Idea abortionists might not kill the idea immediatelyor steal the idea from you, but their goal is to make sure your ideas are neither implemented nor successful. They may speak as if they support your idea, laugh and smile with you, make you think they are helping you, while all the time looking for ways to make your ideas fail. After you have invested some resources into it, after you have gotten to a point where you have an emotional connection to the idea, after you have gotten to a point where you believe it will work, then it dissolves because somebody has worked hard behind to destroy the entire idea and frustrate the idea initiator.

4. ***Idea moderators***: Idea moderators work hard to minimize the scope and size of the idea. They

cannot handle big hairy audacious goals. They work hard to belittle your big dreams, forcing you to make it smaller than it is in reality. They scare you with how it may never succeed at that size, how nobody else has ever tried it and succeeded, how small is beautiful, and why reducing the size of the idea will make it more successful. For instance, you may want to build a duplex, but they will advise you to start first with a two-bedroom bungalow. Idea moderators work hard to distract and discourage you from the big dream you want to accomplish.

5. ***Idea 'stagnators':*** The last negative influencers are idea *'stagnators'*. They may agree with you that the idea is good, are happy with the idea, but they also inform you that the time, environment, or technology is not ripe yet for the idea. Each time you want to take a step to move the idea forward, they say "it's too early", "we are not ready yet", etc. They stagnate you consciously or otherwise as they are scared of either you failing or what will be the outcome of your ideas.

These are the common negative influencers of ideas. Idea initiators meet them all through the cycle of idea metamorphosis – from amorphous concepts to projects, you meet idea killers, idea stealers, idea abortionist, idea moderators, idea stealers, and/or idea stagnators.

Positive Influencers:

> ***1 Samuel 24:20*** [20]***(KJV) And now, behold, I know well that thou shalt surely be king, and that the kingdom of Israel shall be established in thine hand.***

Again, becoming a king in Israel was an idea.

Positive Influencers (PI) are people you should look out for as you work with your ideas. They include;

1. ***Idea facilitators and catalysts***: Idea facilitators and catalysts are individuals that God put in your path to facilitate your ideas and move them from mere ideas to mission, visions, and projects. These are people who are not only happy with your idea but are willing and ready to invest into your idea to ensure it succeeds. Idea facilitators and catalysts go out of their ways to use their personal or private resources – time, money, talent and even networks to support your idea. They will help you understand the nitty-gritty of your idea and process it to profiting.

   Good idea catalysts will not allow you to rest until the idea is turned into a project that will profit you. They will serve as watchdogs, remind you regularly of what you need to do (or decided to do) to move the idea forward and work with you. It is common to hear them as, "How far, have you gone?" "What step have you taken?" If you do not have idea catalyst around you, you might get stagnated in life no matter how beautiful the idea is. Everybody needs such people around them.

2. ***Idea enhancers***: Idea enhancers are idea positive modifiers. They listen to your ideas, meditate over them, improve upon them, and make them better ideas for you. Their tasks and assignments are simple – embellish the idea, fine tune it and enhance the profitability of the idea. Idea enhancers like helping people maximize their ideas and may be paid or not for their work.

3. ***Idea strengtheners & stabilizers:*** Idea strengtheners and stabilizers are another group of positive influencers who work to ensure the stability of your ideas. They also help you to navigate tough segments of your idea processing and implementation. The Bible says: *...the righteous falleth seven times, he riseth again.* You need people who will strengthen you in your hour of need.

Your ideas must go through the metamorphoses of visions, missions, and project to be profitable. In doing that, you must avoid the enemies of metamorphosis (negative influencers) and embrace the friends of metamorphosis (positive influencers).

Interlude 3: Sources and origin of ideas

The mind is the seat of ideas, and a mind without an idea is a barren mind. *Obinna Oleribe*

Wise men put their trust in ideas and not in circumstances. *Ralph Waldo Emerson*

Men's ideas are the direct emanations of their material state. This is true in politics, law, morality, religion etc. *Karl Marx*

A great idea is usually original to more than one discoverer. Great ideas come when the world needs them. They surround the world's ignorance and press for admission. *Austin Phelps*

Creativity is the process of having original ideas that have value. It is a process; it is not random. *Ken Robinson*

To ask at what time a man has first any ideas is to ask when he begins to perceive; having ideas and perception being the same thing. *John Locke*

Chapter 4: IDEA PROCESSES

Ideas rule the world. This is a common saying. However, unprocessed ideas do not rule any world. *It is processed ideas that rule the world.*

Ideas come to you amorphous, they come to you unprocessed. Ideas come to you sometimes as figments of your own imagination. Ideas come to you amoebic in nature, no structure, no shape, no attraction to it. It's only when you have been able to turn that unprocessed idea into a processed idea that you can rule the world in which we live in.

Anyone and everyone can generate ideas, but not anyone and everyone can process ideas and therefore profit from them. Globally, everything you see are products of processed ideas - the air conditioner, light, LED, clothes on your body, toothpaste – they are all products of processed ideas. For instance, in the 19th Century people used sticks or charcoal to clean their teeth. Someone said *this is not good enough,* we can modernize this practice and make something better. Toothbrushes and toothpastes were produced. Over the past several years, we have moved from one brand dominating the market to having different labels of toothpaste in the market.

Life only benefits from ideas that have been processed – fully processed, as only processed ideas can be profitable in life. As not every idea is manageable, profitable, or sellable; you must process your ideas to find out whether it can be profitable.

In processing ideas, you must:

1. **Dream it (and dream it again)**: In *Genesis 37, it was documented, "and Joseph dreamt again"*. You must dream that idea, again and again, you must look at it repeatedly, visualize it repeatedly, and from different angles, different corners, and different points of view. It is in dreaming again that the idea begins to make sense to you. Mark Zuckerberg said, *'No idea can come to you fully formed'*. You have to dream again and again, because what you had as your first dream might not really make sense or be profitable, but ruminating over your dreams makes it form better.

2. **Meditate on it**: The Bible says; *as a man thinketh in his heart so is he*. It also says; *meditate on this thing that thy profiting may appear to all*. Every time you meditate upon an idea, it gets clearer and better. You need to think through the idea. Until you think through an idea, it will not be ready for implementation. It is important to understand that some ideas are for the moment, while others are for the future. For an idea to become a proposal or project and be profitable, you must meditate on it, you must think about it. Friends, sit down with it, relax with it, sleep on it, and dream about it. Let the idea consume you. Regurgitate it from your mind and chew it again and again. If you have written a page about it, re-write it until it is better. Every time a new thought comes into your mind, go ahead and modify, if need be. Keep on modifying

the idea until you get what you really want, or the version that will pay you.

3. **Seek more information on it**: Seek more information about the idea from people, and from books. We are told, and we know, that there is nothing new under heaven. What we see as new are actually the latest versions of the old. Whatever you are seeing now, people have seen and done before. All you have to do is ask questions, what is already in existence? What have people done in that area? Ask questions from idea facilitators, not idea killers. Ask questions from those who can help you achieve your objectives. Read about it, talk about it with the right people, and let them give you a new insight.

When you talk about the ideas you have in your mind, some people will want to kill the idea because it does not make sense to them, but you have a right to decide whether you want to accept their suggestions or not. Talk with someone who can help you clarify your ideas. For instance, when you find a man that you want to marry, do not keep it to yourself; talk to someone about the proposal. If you want to buy something new, talk about it to somebody, and read about it. What are the possible options, how can I make it better?

Many of us have killed several glorious ideas because we just bottled them inside us. What you bottle inside can either consume or destroy you. There are, however, idea killers or stealers. Thus, you must select who you share your ideas with and who gives you advice. You should not talk to everybody about your idea because sometimes it could be destructive.

Seek more information, when you are about doing something you think is new, remember that someone might have done it somewhere else – maybe in a different way. So, what do you do? You pick up what has been done, modify it, and it becomes your own idea. However, if you decide to re-invent the wheel, it may take you ages to achieve. This may actually derail your vision and plans of the idea.

4. **Pray about it**: Remember that the wisdom from above is the highest form of wisdom. You may have done well by yourself, but talk to God about the idea. What does he have to say? Should you pursue? Should you overtake? Will you recover all? God may refuse you pursuing something you think is very wonderful, or ask you to pursue those you did not truly appreciate and value. God is God and He only knows what He has in plans for you. Therefore, talk to God about your ideas in prayer. Why? Because, *it is not by power, it is not by might*.

Of all forms of ideas, revelational ideas are superior to other forms of ideas, and to implement them, you need revelational power which is far ahead of all that you can get from any man or any book. There are many businesses out there which may seem profitable and wonderful, but God may forbid you from venturing into them. If you go ahead, you may end up losing your resources. It is important that you talk to God about your ideas. Do not take this step for granted. It is a critical step in your idea processes. If it is a vision or mission, God must be involved. You can also talk to your spiritual leader(s) about your ideas.

5. **Refine it**: Never get tired of refining your idea until it becomes a profitable idea. When you talk about it, you get new information. Therefore, speak, learn and refine and refine. When you talk to God about it, use His instructions and guidance to further refine your idea. When you read about it, go ahead and refine.

    An idea must be refined and re-defined until it becomes a perfect idea for what you want to achieve.

6. **Pilot it:** We will be speaking more on this in the next two chapters on Idea implementation.

Interlude 4: Purpose of idea

Ideas give direction to life and purpose to pursuit. *Obinna Oleribe*

Ideas are burden to the bearer, but profitable to the user. *Obinna Oleribe*

Chapter 5: IDEA IMPLEMENTATION

You will recall that the essence of ideas is to solve problems, and by solving problems we make profits. You will also recall that in marketing ideas, the 7Ps of marketing mix are critical – products, place, people, price, promotion, packaging and promotion. Now, having known what ideas are, and understood the key essence and modalities of ideas, it is time to talk about **idea implementation**. I will be introducing what I have called The Idea Implementation Cycle (TIIC). This cycle will be unveiling ideas from a different perspective.

Exodus 25:40 (KJV) ***And look that thou make them after their pattern, which was shewed thee in the mount.***

It is advised that we do everything according to a defined pattern. To succeed in any area or issue of life, there is a pattern and we must follow the pattern or sweat some more.

For instance, to succeed in getting a young girl to marry, to build a house, or start a business, there are patterns to follow. To succeed with any idea that may come to you in life, there is a pattern to implement it. And not going with the pattern will lead or result in pain, and many have been pained, battered and beaten because they left the pattern that was there to be followed. And any time you leave the pattern, you end in pain.

For instance, people have spent a lot of resources to build houses, some a four to five storey house; and by the time they finish building, everything collapses because the relevant architectural and structural patterns for building were not followed. Many buy vehicles, drive because they think they know how to drive, and by the time it is a few months, they have destroyed the car via single or multiple accidents, just because the pattern of driving was not followed.

So, in looking at The Idea Implementation Cycle (TIIC), I will share with you the 7Ps of TIIC.

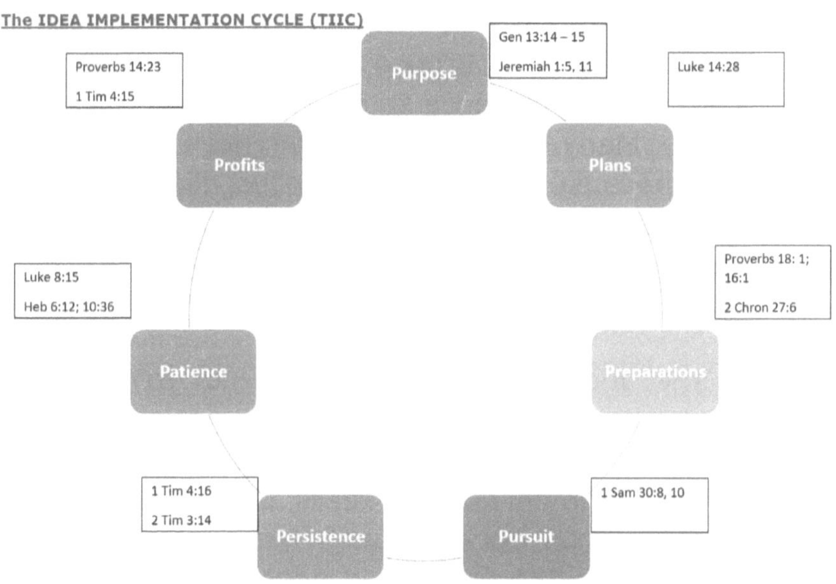

Purpose: Every idea has a purpose for which it was generated. To succeed with any God given idea, the purpose must be in alignment with your personal purpose. If there is a misalignment between the purpose of the idea and the purpose of your life, implementation becomes a struggle. No matter how good the idea is, if the purpose for which you are working and running with the idea is not in alignment with your personal purpose, then implementation becomes a major struggle.

Let me expand. As I said previously, the essence of ideas is to solve problems. But understand that you are not created to solve all problems; you are created to solve a particular kind or type of problem. It is this problem that defines your purpose.

Jeremiah 1:5 (KJV), says *"Before I formed thee in the belly I knew thee; and before thou camest forth out of the womb I sanctified thee, and I ordained thee a prophet unto the nations"*. There is a purpose for which you were made, created and for which you exist today, and friends, you must identify that purpose and align with ideas that is directed to your purpose to be able to run the ideas successfully. Many have developed or received excellent ideas, but because the ideas are not in alignment with their purposes, they could not implement them. So, for your ideas to be successful, their purposes must align with your purposes.

It takes the understanding of a thing not to abuse it. Many people have lost it because they do not understand the concept of purpose. For instance, if a person decides to come to work in only under-wears, people will mistake him/her to be mad because under-wears are primarily designed to serve the purpose of undercover. There is a purpose for everything under heaven; there is a purpose for a man and that of a woman. The trend in the advanced world today where a man tries to function like a woman and vice versa is against nature.

The idea implementation cycle begins with the understanding of the concept of purpose. This brings us to the second P of the idea implementation cycle - the P of PLANNING.

Planning: Proper planning prevents poor performance. Benjamin Franklin supposedly once said, "If you fail to plan, you are planning to fail." Ideas are never implemented successfully without proper planning. It requires adequate time-out to plan to be able to effectively implement a good idea. Ideas don't fail because they are bad; rather ideas fail because people did not adequately plan for them. Luke 14:28 (KJV) says, *"For which of you, intending to build a tower, sitteth not down first, and counteth the cost, whether he have sufficient to finish it?"*

Planning affects you in all areas of life. For instance, if you did not plan for what to wear to office, you may come in on a Monday morning looking tattered or even arrive late. Some of us think of what to wear to office a night before, we should also plan for what we will do within the week, next month and so forth. Similarly, with ideas, if we must implement them successfully, we must plan for them. Don't just think that ideas are ad-hoc events. No, they are not. They require significant time, mental and physical energy for planning. In planning, one needs to look at those 7Ps stated in the previous chapter. The P of product – what am I producing? What product is linked to my idea? The P of place – where will I implement it? The P of price – how much will it cost me? And how much will people be willing to pay for my product? The P of people – who am I producing for? And who will I produce with? As well as the Ps of promotion, packaging and production. At the planning stage, the 7Ps come together to give you an awesome result.

It is vital, at the planning stage to answer the six plus two questions of life – why am I doing this? What am I producing? How will I go about it? How much will it cost me? Who will I work with? Who will I make it for? Where will I do it? And when will I start? It takes planning to think through the entire process. Planning allows for proper meditation around the idea. Planning allows you to think and meditate over the idea.

No idea will ever be successfully implemented without proper planning! Why? Because *proper planning prevents poor performance*. Actually, *prior proper planning prevents painfully poor production*. For instance, when you earn your salary, without proper planning, you misuse your money, and will be broke before the next pay day. Planning prevents pain, sweating, and shame. It takes a long time to plan a good speech, a good lecture and a good presentation. If you are not performing to your highest level, it could be because you did not plan well for it!

If your idea must succeed, you must plan for it. Likewise, if your marriage must succeed, you must plan for it; if your career must advance, plan for it; and if your finances must move forward, you must plan. Life is all about planning. Remember, when you fail to plan, you have planned to fail.

As you plan and align your vision to your purpose, you will not fail. Go home remembering that proper planning prevents poor performance (5Ps). God will help us to plan well.

When we have established the purpose of our ideas and made plans for them, the next step is to prepare for their implementation. This brings us to the third P in the implementation cycle, the P of preparation.

Preparation: The bible talks about preparation in **2 Chronicles 27:6 (KJV)** where it says *"Jothan became mighty because he prepared his ways before the Lord His God"*. Mighty destiny is a function of prolonged and adequate preparation. You cannot be mighty if you did not prepare for it. I say in most of my trainings on leadership, "You can be big without thinking great; but you cannot be great without thinking big."

No one can become mighty by accident. To become mighty in life, you must make adequate preparations. Bible asked that who amongst you will want to build a tower without first sitting down and counting the cost – that is preparation. The wise man did a foundation and built his house upon a solid foundation, but the fool built his own on the ground so that when the rain came, one stood and the other fell. Preparation makes the difference.

When your life has no solid foundation, it means that you did not prepare for it which implies that you will not go far. Many of us are stagnated in life not because Satan is strong, but because we have not given ourselves adequate preparation. People think that the issues of life are just questions of who you know and who you don't know. That is not the complete truth my friends, prepare yourselves.

Opportunities do come to us, but most times we are not prepared for them. So, to implement ideas, preparation is fundamental.

According to **Proverbs 16:1,** God will never prepare for you. No matter how many years you pray, fast and make sacrifices to God, God will never prepare for you, you know why? Because **Proverbs 16:1 (NKJV)** says that *"the preparation of the heart belong to man, but* *the answer of the tongue is from the Lord".* Preparation belongs to man.

Every man is ordained by heaven and is commanded by God and by our destinies to prepare. You know why people fail exams; or why many ideas can never succeed - lack of preparation. We know that adequate preparation prevents poor performance! Another way to put it is that proper preparation prevents perspiration (4P). Many are sweating and perspiring on daily basis because there is no proper preparation prior to their current assignment implementation. The preparation of the heart belongs to man.

For instance, if you want to get married, build a house, run a vision, or achieve a goal, prepare for it. With time always on the move, what are you doing to ensure your dreams are not wasted?

To succeed in any area of life, or to succeed with any idea that God has given you, preparation is important. Jothan became mighty not because he loved the Lord, gave offering, went to church, or that somebody helped him; but because he prepared his ways. If you want to become mighty in life, understand that preparation is your primary access to it. Show me a man that is always passing his exams with a score of 90% and above, and you will see a man who is always prepared. Any idiot can get a score of 90% or more once in a while, but to come first in class consistently, preparation is required. What I am saying is simple. In life, you can succeed by chance once, but to be successful in every adventure of your life requires adequate preparation.

Ideas can be successfully implemented only when there is adequate preparation. That is why **Proverbs 18:1** says that *through* desire, a man prepares for the greatness of his entire life. So, you are not compelled to prepare, you desire to prepare. It is a product of your innermost being. Truth is that nothing great and good happens by accident. Some ideas that we celebrate today took people several years of preparation, some took up to 10 or 20 years of preparation. For instance, the man who invented the light bulbs (Thomas Edison) tried 1000 times and failed over 999 times before he discovered the right way. An idea that succeeds or will be successfully implemented requires adequate preparation.

Preparation is like a foundation and the Bible says; "if the foundation be destroyed, what can the righteous do?" Similarly, if there are no preparations, what can the idea owner do? So, your righteousness does not replace your preparative activities. For instance, a pastor who goes to preach without preparation and hopes that God will put words in his mouth will talk nonsense. For it is good to prepare what you want to preach, so that even if something changes, at least you have a guideline. Preparation is required for the successful delivery of any idea. So, what are the five fundamental components of preparation?

Desire: You must desire that the idea will succeed, and so desire to invest your resources in preparation. Why? Because, preparation is expensive. For instance, to go to work, some of you took your baths; applied cream; ironed your cloths; wore perfume and these are not cheap. To come to office before 8.00am requires preparation and the reason some people come late to office every morning is because they did not prepare the previous night. You cannot prepare effectively without the right state of desire.

Decide: When you have the right desire, then decide on what steps to take. Some of us here have desired to own a house in Abuja. Now is the time to make a decision. Every idea requires decision to be effectively operational. Your lack of decision is actually a decision against you. If you didn't take any decision at all, you have decided deliberately against yourself and against your desire. You desire and decide and then prepare for it. Some of you planning to travel abroad should understand that there are some basic requirements like IELTS, GMAT or GRE exams. If you are serious, you should decide on it and prepare for it.

Determination: Decision without determination is equalled to destruction. You must determine that nothing will stop you from achieving your objective and implementing your ideas. For instance, you desire to marry a wife, you decide on it, and even when she says "No" to you severally, you determine not to give in until you make her your wife. This is the same with ideas. There will be obstacles. There will be challenges. But friends, you have all it takes to overcome the obstacles and challenges if you will determine never to quit but to stay on until success is guaranteed.

Devotion: To succeed in this stage of idea implementation, you must devote your time, resources, intellect and energy to achieving it. It is important to note that devotion is not only about "morning devotion", there is more to devotion than having a morning devotion. Every idea that must succeed must enjoy your full devotion. Some people that you see as successful devoted their lives (most times) to only one idea. For instance, Bill Gates and Steve Jobs devoted their lives to Microsoft and Apple respectively. Don't be jack of all trades and master of none. Devotion is critical to your success in life.

Dependence on Divine help: This is the most important of all requirements towards effective and adequate preparation, because by strength shall no man prevail. It is not by power nor by might but by the power of the Holy Spirit. The book of Psalm 146:3 (KJV) says *"thou shall not put thy trust in princes, nor in a son of man, in whom there is no help,* and verse 5 *(NKJV)* says *"happy is he who has the God of Jacob for his help, whose hope is in the Lord his God who made heaven and earth".* So, when your help comes from God, then your success is guaranteed. Depend on Divine helps.

So, let's remember to put our ideas into reality through hard work, planning, taking necessary steps, talking to the right people, and above all depending on your maker to help you have your ideas implemented. Remember when you fail plan to plan, you plan to fail. Was it not W.J Cameron who said, 'money never starts an idea, it is the idea that starts the money'? Hard work begets success. If you dream about an idea, you work for it.

Ideas are great only when you prepare for them. It is time to prepare for that idea applying these simple 5Ds of preparation. When you do so, you will surely make a mark in life in the name of Jesus. If you want a successful goal, career, destiny, or a successful idea implemented, then you must prepare for it. Where there are no preparations, there is a lot of perspiration.

With adequate preparation come PURSUIT.

PURSUIT: This skill is most critical because plans not pursued can never result in profiting. It takes deliberate pursuit of a plan to realize the expectations of the plan irrespective of your investments in the plan and its preparations. For instance, if you plan on getting married this year, if you don't 'pursue' a lady, you may never get married. If you plan on buying a car, start saving and looking for extra means of income, otherwise, you may end up not buying a car. If you want to obtain a degree, if you don't start seeking admission, you will never achieve your desire.

Every issue of life, beyond planning and preparation, requires that you take deliberate steps to pursue it. 1Samuel 30:8 (KJV) says ***"And David enquired at the Lord, saying, Shall I pursue after this troop? shall I overtake them? And he answered him, Pursue: for thou shalt surely overtake them, and without fail recover all"***. When you have asked of God, planned, done the necessary preparations, and God has answered you, it is then time to take steps in pursuing the idea, despite how faithful and good God is to you, you will have little or no testimonies without proper and purposeful pursuit.

For instance, every time we pray, God answers. But for us to see the results we must take steps in line with our prayers, because God will only help those that are ready to take steps. God said in His word that the hand that lays the foundation will complete it. The spirit of God will only partner with you to do the work.

In pursuing your vision, plans, and ideas; the DRA principles (Do, Review and Act) concept is critical and must be implemented.

Do: Many of us are good at talking, but very poor at doing. Some have wonderful ideas in their heads and can speak about it for years but are very bad at doing. One of the things that hinder us from doing is the spirit of procrastination. Most people wait for when the time is right and everything we need is ready, but friends, everything cannot be ready because the enemy (devil) of your destiny is constantly at work and at war. For instance, if you are looking for a perfect man or lady that has all the qualities you need, you will never get married. This is why, **Doing** is critical, and you must step out of your comfort zone and step into doing.

It is not money you need, but the courage to do it. Many of us want to build a house, but have not even taken the steps to look for a land; or do you intend building the house on your head? Some want to be wealthy, but prefer to save their money in the bank. They bought into the lie that the bank is a safe place to keep their monies. What they do not know is that saving money in the bank makes your money to lose value over time. The bank will only give you an interest every month which will never be compared to what they make by recycling your resources. Have you ever heard of time value for money?

The land on which I first built a house in Abuja was gotten for free because I took a bold step. I got an interpreter, visited a community chief, and shared my vision concerning building and establishing a hospital for the community. The Chief agreed and asked me to make a choice of any portion of the land I wanted and that was how I got to build the hospital and my first house. So, doing is critical to your success. After doing, the next step is to review.

Review: When you begin to take steps, don't be that person that keeps going straight without looking back or stopping for a while to review his/her steps. You need to pause, reflect, and review by asking some questions such as: Am I taking steps in the right direction, am I doing the right things, am I working for the right results, am

I working with the right people, am I in the right place, am I working with the right strategies? etc. Many people are moving around in circles, sweating profusely as the days, month and years pass by, believing they are making progress when actually they are fully stagnated. Are you one of them? They may think they are making profit or progress, when actually they are not. That you are in motion does not mean you are making progress.

Regular review results in refined strategies and sustained progress. Learn to review your works. If you are a farmer, trader, mechanic, doctor, nurse, programmer, fashion designer, politician, etc., review your work. Learn to review your works and progress at defined points in your life. When you review yourself regularly, people won't review you negatively as you must have identified your mistakes and errors, and made adequate corrections before other people see them. After the review, act on your findings.

Act: When you have reviewed yourself, career, idea, family, or work and have done an honest personal check, there are things you will find that are not right and therefore you need to act on them to correct them. Review without the appropriate desire and willingness to act on outcomes and findings is time wasted. You act to modify, to change, or to make them better. You must be willing to take steps to make corrections and to take steps to modify the errors to make your ideas work.

The above is the DRA concept which is critical in the pursuit of ideas. In pursuing, you don't just pursue as a blind man but you learn to Do, Review and Act. To succeed in idea implementation strategies, apply the DRA concept. For instance, every Monday morning as you appear in the office, review your last week's work, identify your mistakes and develop strategies to correct them.

In reviewing, you find things that are working that you will continue to do, things that are not working that you will have to stop, and things that ought to work that you are not doing yet and have to start doing immediately. It takes a complete implementation of the DRA concept to get the results you desire.

One of the greatest enemies of success is blaming people for your failure. Yes, there could be forces against you but friends, as long as you are projecting your problem you will never have the capacity to handle it. It is necessary for us to look inward, internalize our problems, and decide to solve them by asking the following questions: What can I do? and what can I do to make a change in this problem I am in? When you answer these questions, before you know it, you will get the courage to take steps and there will be a change in your life.

After aligning the purpose of the idea to your personal purpose, planning, preparation and pursuit; you must persist until victory is achieved. This is the next P in this cycle - Persistence.

Persistence: Many of us do very well to start, many do well at planning, preparation and pursuit, but very few persist until profit is achieved. I am sure that most of what you have in life were not gotten overnight, you persisted. For instance, you got your certificates – first and second degree – because you persisted; you won those awards and accolades because you persisted, you got your wife to agree to marry you because you persisted, you learned that skill and went on to become an expert because you persisted, you even learned how to cook, drive or dive because you persisted.

Also, when a woman gets pregnant, she must persist with the pregnancy for nine months before she can deliver a mature healthy child. If she is in a hurry to have a child and decides to bring the baby out before three months are over, that would be an abortion. If the baby comes out at seven months, that would be a premature (preterm). If she wants the preterm baby to survive, she will have to spend a lot of money in incubator and oxygen care, and sometimes for antibiotics and steroids. But if the woman carries the baby for nine months, she may deliver and on the same day, leave the hospital because she persisted till the end. Good results come to those who have purpose, who plan, who prepare, who pursue, who persist and who wait patiently.

So, there are three fundamental Cs in idea implementation as regards persistence - **Commencement, Continuity and Completion**. There is a grace to start something (commence), there is another grace to continue, and there is a different grace to work till completion. Many of us have started on so many ideas, but we have lost it along the line because we didn't have that capacity and grace to either continue or complete what we started. That is, we lack the grace to persist until we complete the project. For instance, laying a foundation for a house is good, but no one lives in the foundation. People have to allow the house to be built from the foundation to the roofing and completion before they can move into it.

Ideas have similar challenges. That you have begun well does not mean you will end well. You have to persist to get to your planned destination. That you entered school and matriculated, does not guarantee you a certificate of graduation. You have to stay four or more years as the case may be to be able to complete your journey and then wear your graduation gown. Not everyone that matriculates, graduates. Experience has shown that many matriculate, but only a very few graduate. Let me reemphasize, that you have begun a process like schooling, does not mean you will complete it, except you persist. That you joined the public health world does not mean you will make a mark in it, except you are willing to persist in it.

That you have a good idea for 2018 does not mean you will profit from it except you are willing to persist in its development and implementation. It is important therefore that you do not get wearied on the way. Do not allow your yesterday's works to be in vain by quitting or giving up at your eleventh hour. Allow the spirit of persistence to go to work in you and through you.

Every man who is married, for instance, will understand that it is not the first day you wooed your wife that she agreed. You despised the shame of her refusal, went to her over and over again, and persistence on your part until she agreed. So, persistence is important. Many have lost their miracles at the eleventh hour, they worked so hard, they tried, they struggled, and when it was time for them to begin to reap, they gave up. It will not be our portion to give up in our careers, businesses, finances, love life, etc. in Jesus name. If you have started anything good and worthwhile, please do not quit. *However, if you are doing the wrong thing, you should quit immediately.* If you are in the wrong direction, quit. But if you are on the right track, persist.

If you are on a course or a program, do not quit saying it is difficult; people have been where you are right now, and they succeeded. If you are trying to learn a skill, don't quit because it is becoming tougher. The day becomes darkest before dawn. There are things that could come to you not on a platter of gold, but when you acquire them, they become gold in your hands. That is what persistence does. If you want to buy a land in Abuja and you have not found one, persist. If you have found land and you are building a house and things are getting tougher, persist.

In building a house, you can build by direct labour instead of by contract, to make things cheaper and easier for you. You can buy 100 pieces of block every month and store them until you have enough blocks to build. Do you know that a thousand blocks can build a Boys Quarter? Don't allow anybody to tell you that you cannot build a house. For instance, the first house I built here in Abuja was a mud house; I lived there, made money there, and found my wife while living there. But friends, I am no longer there. I have left it long ago. Just start from where you are.

It is not where you are that matters. Do not define yourself by where you are, define yourself by where you are going. Don't define yourself by your current position; define yourself by your future destination. Don't define yourself by your present challenges, define yourself by your future accomplishments. You know the truth, you will never get **there** if you don't start from **here**. A wise man says the difference between here and there is T and that T is time. But time can only be relevant to you if you maximize it. If you gaze at time and believe that you have time, the time will be wasted, and nothing will change.

Friends, persist. James 1:25 (NKJV) says **"But he who looks into the perfect law of liberty and continues in it and is not a forgetful hearer but a doer of the work, this one will be blessed in what he does"**. So, it is not looking that makes you blessed, but it is continuing therein. 1 Timothy 4:15 (NKJV) says ***"Meditate on these things, give yourself entirely to them, that your progress may be evident to all."*** This means that you should persist in that which you are doing till your profiting appears.

Profit is a reality, but it is not a gift. Success is also a reality, but again, it is not a gift. Everyone wants to succeed, but it is not a prayer point, but a work point. And one of the work points is persistence in what you are doing.

Let us take a look at the last component of the idea implementation cycle - patience.

Patience: This is one virtue that many believers are lacking so much these days as people find it difficult to understand why things happen. In this season of fast food, fast trains, fast cars, fast computers, fast services, etc., patience is no longer a critical virtue as people want their desires met now and here. Most times we desire the good testimonies of people that we hear of in church, but we are not willing to pay the price they paid – including the price of patience. Imagine a pregnant woman who loses patience and decides to deliver her baby at five or six months. She will have to pay more money to keep the baby alive.

There are two basic requirements to obtaining a divine promise – Faith and Patience. The Bible said we should avoid anything that distracts us but run the race of life with patience. Also, it advices us that after we have done everything that God has commanded us to do, there is one more thing to be done which is to be patient and allow God to take control.

Luke 8:15 (KJV) says ***"But that on the good ground are they, which in an honest and good heart, having heard the word, keep it, and bring forth fruit with patience"***.

Because we live in a world of fast food, fast snacks, fast cars, fast internet, fast everything, we are losing this virtue of patience. Patience is no longer a flower that grows in everybody's garden. You can go to a tailor or a bakery and ask for a dress or cake to be made for you in 24 hours and it will be done. This has its consequences.

In idea implementation, patience is a virtue. In every department of your life, be it in your relationships, families, work positions, partnership, patience is needed. In implementing any idea – educational, technological, ministerial, health, financial, etc., we need patience. Patience is not a gift from God, but part of the fruits of the Holy Spirit.

Recall that fruits are not produced over night, but outcomes of detailed and time-consuming endeavours. Just as having a tree in your compound does not mean you have fruits, similarly, being baptized by the Holy Ghost does not mean you have the fruit of the Spirit including patience. To obtain fruits, we need to cultivate the tree - manure and water it, weed around it, protect it from wild animals, and after a while harvest the fruits. That is why there are people who are baptized with the Holy Spirit without having any of the fruits in them: no joy, peace, patience, gentleness, etc. as documented in the bible (Galatians 5:22). As not every tree you plant bears fruit, not everyone with the Spirit has fruit.

Patience is one virtue that is cultivated. You just have to learn how to be patient and give yourself time. Time is a healer of all problems. Everyone is on their own personal race. We need patience to bear fruits. Many of us have destroyed our fruitful capacities by lack of patience. People want to finish even before they start; but that is not how it works. Patience is required in every journey of your life. Patience is in your personal lives, otherwise you will have avoidable battles to fight every day. You need patience with people, systems, organizations, as well as in implementing that idea in your mind. Many have aborted good ideas or good programmes because they lacked patience.

Many of us have failed to succeed because of impatience. Either because we quit very early or expect results too fast as the evident manifestation of impatience is quitting. Today we live in the world of quitters. People quit from school, jobs, marriages, or ideas because they think it is not working. Many are experts in starting and quitting and starting again. But this is retrogressive. It is like planting trees and uprooting them to replant them somewhere else. To bear fruits, the trees have to stay in a place long enough. Frequently uprooting the tree hinders fruit production. Some people are like that, uproot themselves and plant themselves on regular basis. As they keep uprooting themselves, yes there could be some instant gratification, but these are not long lasting and may result in some avoidable consequences.

Show me a man that has successfully implemented an idea and made a name in life and you will notice they have been in that particular position/career long enough to make a name. For instance, people like Bishop David Oyedepo, Bill Gates, Michael Jordan, Barack Obama, etc. are all known – but for one thing. Nobody ever makes a name doing one million things at once.

Learn patience and cultivate patience. Let those who have the Holy Ghost in them allow the Spirit to bear fruit in them. Many may speak in tongues, but there are no fruit in them because they have not been able to cultivate the virtue of patience to be able to bear good fruits.

Patience is required to bring forth fruits. When you have paid your price in any idea, job, or activity, cultivate patience and wait for your rewards. When you exercise patience, good things come your way. Patience does not defile hope but waters your hope. The only thing that defiles hope is YOU. You are the greatest enemy of your hope. Hope is personal and private.

Interlude 5: Burden of idea

One of the greatest pains to human nature is the pain of a new idea. *Walter Bagehot*

The idea is in thyself the impediment too in thyself. *Thomas Carlyle*

There is no hard times for good ideas. *H. Gordon Selfridge*

Ideas are easy, implementation is hard. *Guy Kawasaki*

Ideas are easy, it is the execution of ideas that really separates the sheep from the goats. *Sue Grafton*

Whenever ideas fail men, intent words. *Martin H. Fischer*

We are healthy only to the extent that our ideas are humane. *Kurt Vonnegut JR.*

You shouldn't be a prisoner of your own ideas. *Sol Lewitt*

Running with an idea produces pain, but the outcomes deliver gain. *Obinna Oleribe*

Chapter 6: POWER OF PROTECTION

Life is full of challenges. One thing that everyone must face at a certain time in life is the attack of wickedness. The Bible in Psalm 20:1 (KJV) says ***"The Lord hear thee in the day of trouble; the name of the God of Jacob defend thee".*** Understand that something will attack your ideas, vision and/or programme as there are agents that have been programmed by hell and devil to attack you, whether you like it or not.

Abraham was met by God at the age of seventy-five. At that time, he was a barren man and God declared that he would have a child. But he continued as a barren man for another 25 years before the promise was fulfilled. Joseph had a beautiful dream at about the age of fifteen and it took him another fifteen solid years during which he suffered various attacks – pit, servant-hood, prison, etc. before he climbed the throne. David was made a king by Samuel, but he had to fight Saul and several forces of wickedness for several years before he ended up as king of Israel.

Friends, the journey to the top is not a straight line. Anybody that told you that success is simple lied to you. Success is never a straight line. Achieving your life ambition and dreams is never a straight line. Getting your ideas into profiting is never a straight line. There are bound to be several challenges and attacks. But your responsibility is to keep your vineyard. Many have missed it in life because at the slightest challenge, they backed out. The funny thing at times is that for the things that are not so important, we stay put; but for the things that are important, we back out so easily.

There is this story of a young lady who got married, and after a while got pregnant and later had a miscarriage. She was counselled and was told to pray and fast. This she did and after a few years got pregnant again, gave birth and then testified about it. But many of us have given up on our ideas following the slightest miscarriage or challenges. If we have the slightest challenge in our academics, we stop. When we have small challenge in our marriages, we back out. Friends, there is no life without challenges, we must learn to keep our vineyards.

Many people are good at advising others on how they can do better, helping them keep their vineyards, but their own vineyards they have not or cannot keep. Some of us have the best ideas on how things can work, but, we cannot apply them to ourselves.

Our own vineyards, we have not kept. This is so common amongst us. Many think that the only way to grow is to go abroad – London, America, Canada, South Africa, Ghana, Kenya, Russia, Germany, etc. Friends, there is nowhere life is easy. If you cannot do well in Nigeria, you may not do well elsewhere. Do not be deceived, Nigeria may have its challenges, but Nigeria still remains the easiest place to succeed.

Nigeria is a place where the policies and procedures are for you. For instance, you can open a shop in front of your compound with minimal disturbances. But, try it elsewhere and see what would happen. Before you get a license to be a *vulcaniser,* cobbler or a mechanic, you have to go through several processes and pay several bills. That is why many people currently abroad want to come back home. Many live in debts over there – and to them, it is normal. Here you buy cars, build houses, and go to school without debt. But it is not the same everywhere. Friends, protect your vineyards.

You can succeed while you are here. But how can you succeed, you must identify what contribution you want to make in life. Life is all about contributions.

Many of us are living on the realms of consumptions. Consuming can never make you successful in life. You have to make contributions. No one becomes relevant in life by consuming – give me, pay me, dash me - you can never make it that way! Nothing anybody gives you can ever make you succeed. It can serve as a seed, but you need to plant the seed to become successful. Every gift is just for a moment. Who you become in life is dependent on what you do with yourself – keep your vineyards.

Protect your ideas, protect your visions, and do not allow little distractions to push you aside or make you quit. Friends, there is no one who have succeeded today who did not go through various challenges, I mean major challenges. We celebrate Jesus. That is good. But, He died and He rose up from the dead after three days. Was it easy to die? Can you go through what He went through? The mother of James and John wanted her sons on the right and left sides of Jesus. Jesus asked "Are ye able to drink of the cup that I shall drink of, and to be baptized with the baptism that I am baptized with?" (Matt 20:22 KJV)

You want to be like Moses or Abraham, can you go through what they went through in life? Abraham was in his old age, God said circumcise yourself and all your male children. And Bible said, same day he did so without anaesthesia. Try it now and you will see what it feels like. Some may want to be like David Oyedepo or Faith Oyedepo. Can you be a wife to Bishop Oyedepo? Understand that to be a wife to him is a huge sacrifice. Friends, there is nobody who becomes anything in life without paying a price, protect your vineyard.

Many of you are too careless and nonchalant with life, allowing anything that shall be to be, *que sera sera*. That is not right!

The entire world is programmed for random movement. For instance, if you cook delicious soup today and do not refrigerate it within a day or two, it will sour. If you wake up in the morning without taking your bath, you will smell. If you close your mouth for three hours without opening it, you will have mouth odour. Things are programmed to get spoilt by natural means. It takes orderliness and constant protection not to get spoilt. The same way you take care of yourself, waking up, taking your bath and spending some hours to beautify yourself, also take some time to protect your visions, ideas and your programs.

Learn to protect your destiny, your work and assignments. Like it is said, twenty children will not play together for twenty years. As classmates or playmates, if something happens to any of you, it will not stop the others from moving on, writing their exams, and living their lives. You will only be missed for seconds to minutes, and thereafter be referred to as in the past - Late. Even at workplaces, people may resume work same day but everyone came as individuals. Therefore, keep your vineyard, protect your vineyards, preserve your vineyard and ensure that your work packages, assignments, ideas, or visions are done and protected.

Therefore, do not ever allow the challenges of this world to derail your vision. Do not be too busy to overlook your vineyard. Do not be like the man in 1 Kings 20 who was given an assignment by the king to keep a man, and while the young man was busy "here and there" in vs 40, the man in his custody.

Many are not keeping or protecting their vineyards. Keep your vineyards to be able to celebrate your vineyard and eat the fruits thereof. Protect your ideas, visions and dreams.

Interlude 6: Gains of processed ideas

Positivity and progressively processing ideas change the world. *Obinna Oleribe*

The more an idea is developed, the more concise becomes its expression; the more a tree is pruned, the better is the fruit. *Alfred Bougeart*

The rewards in business go to the man who does something with an idea. *William Benton*

There is one thing stronger than all the armies in the world, and that is an idea whose time has come. *Victor Hugo*

So long as new ideas are created, sales will continue to reach new highs *Charles F. Kettering*

But the truth is, it's not the idea, it's never the idea, it's always what you do with it. *Neil Gaiman*

All big things in this world are done by people who are naïve and have an idea that is obviously impossible. *Charles Hamilton*

All achievements, all earned riches have their beginning in an idea. *Napoleon Hill*

We don't let them have ideas, why would we let them have guns. *Joseph Stalin*

Idea not designed to solve life problems is never profitable. *Obinna Oleribe*

Chapter 7: TURNING YOUR IDEAS INTO PROJECTS

Any idea that is not turned into a project is a wasted idea. Isaiah 5:1 KJV says **"now will I sing to my well-beloved a song of my beloved touching his vineyard. My well-beloved hath a vineyard in a very fruitful hill"**. Understand, therefore, that for one to be anyone's beloved, s/he must have a vineyard. Every human being is ordained by God to nurse a garden. Your ideas will only remain an imagination in your head until you transform that idea into a project and that project is your vineyard.

Vineyards are not functions of how much money you have, but your willingness to take steps. I am challenging you to use whatever you have now to start a vineyard. You can use as little as few dollars to start a vineyard. There are so many divine opportunities around where we live; we can look for one and turn it into a vineyard. You can even give your mother in the village a little money to start a low-cost business for you.

With a few dollars, you can start a project. Look around your neighbourhoods, there is a need you can meet. Friends, I am telling you, no matter how much you are paid as salary, it can never satisfy all your needs. It is not wise for us to buy vegetables in the market when we have uncultivated farmlands around where we live and work. If you can turn a small container in your house into a fish pond, you can have enough fish to eat on monthly basis. If you can use ten or twenty blocks and make a fish pond and put tiles on it, you will have an additional stream of income.

We complain a lot because we don't maximize capital to own our own vineyards. Therefore, my charge to you is to start your own vineyards. Will you always succeed, No! Isaiah 5:2 KJV says ***"And he fenced it, and gathered out the stones thereof, and planted it with the choicest vine, and built a tower in the midst of it, and also made a winepress therein: and he looked that it should bring forth grapes and it brought forth wild grapes"***.

We have been so good castigating others who are doing something while we waste our time doing nothing. It is time we get ourselves engaged in something tangible. "... ***my well-beloved concerning his vineyard***...", ***his*** and not ***our*** vineyard is stressed. Some people are waiting for their fathers to die to inherit their property. Yes, he will die someday. But do you know that your father may die and Will his property to other people? Now that you are young, start your own vineyard.

I built my first hospital with mud blocks, now I have a hospital with real blocks. I started my first pharmacy shop in a container; today I have a real pharmacy store on block walls. In my house I have a small portion where we plant vegetable, I always feel happy when I see people going there to cut vegetables to put in my food. It is not big, but it is a good beginning. The garden was deliberately planned into the landscaping. You just have to start somewhere.

Today, if you don't have any additional source of income or what will save you money on monthly basis, you are not doing well. There are things you should not be buying every week/month. There are things you can do that will fetch money. Evaluate your environment and see what they need but lack – and provide it. Do a proper market analysis to ensure that you provide it at the appropriate price and quantity/quality. This way, your neighbours will buy from you. If you only buy from people and have nothing to sell to people, you are in trouble – you are a waster.

Life is a function of networks; if you are not interconnected, you are wasting. Our lives can be better if we can transform our ideas into projects. If you have a good voice, use it; if you can write, write; and if you can teach, teach. Some of you can teach evening classes to small children after office hours. Use it.

Begin now to put your ideas into projects. You don't need to buy a land to farm, you can borrow or hire or even be favoured with one. You don't need to buy a land to start a business; you can talk to a landowner, and ask him to allow you set up a container or temporary structure. Then stock up the container with few things – even on credit, and pay back as you sell. But don't be a thief in your vineyard. Do not begin on a wrong foundation, do not steal or cheat.

You can start a snail farm. Just plant two plantain trees and throw few snails into them and in six to 12 months' time, harvest. You will be amazed at how many snails you harvest. These simple things do not require expertise. Also, if you know someone that owns a poultry, you can ask to put a few dollars into it and partner with him/her. Do not finish the money in your account now.

According to Parkinson's law, when people get extra money, they misuse it. Invest your extra income into something so that anytime you remember what you did with it, you will be very proud. Be forward looking and consciously move forward. Even though it may appear slow, move forward. Start your vineyard. If you are single, you can save more. Do not be a waster!

Genesis 2:10 KJV says "***And a river went out of Eden to water the garden; and from thence it was parted, and became into four heads***". God gives you a primary source of income. However, that income should open up new income sources. If we cut off so many of our excesses, we will be amazed at how much we will save.

Friends start your vineyard now. Let me, in the second part of this book show why entrepreneurship is critical and vital to us all.

Interlude 7: Pathway of idea

Ideas first appear as raw materials; when processed, they become finished products. *Obinna Oleribe*

Money never starts an idea; it is the idea that starts the money. *W.J Cameron*

So many new ideas are at first strange and horrible though ultimately valuable that a very heavy responsibility rests upon those who would prevent their dissemination. *John B.S Haldane*

Ideas lose themselves as quickly as quail and one must wing them the minute they rise out of the grass or they are gone. *Thomas F. Kennedy*

Although words exist for the most part for the transmission of ideas, there are some which produce such violent disturbance in our feelings that the role they play in the transmission of ideas is lost in the background. *Albert Einstein*

An idea must not be condemned for being a little shy and incoherent; all new ideas are shy when introduced first among our old ones. We should have patience and see whether the incoherency is likely to wear off or to wear on, in which latter case the sooner we get rid of them the better. *Samuel Butler*

There are two things that have to happen before an idea catches on. One is that the idea should be good. The other is that it should fit in with the temper of the age. If it does not, even a good idea may well be passed by. *Jawaharial Nehu*

Now ideas are the raw materials of progress. Everything first takes shape in the form of an idea. But an idea by itself is worth nothing. An idea is like a machine, must have power applied to it before it can accomplish anything. The men who have won fame and fortune through having an idea are those who developed every ounce of their strength and every dollar they could muster to putting it into operation. Ford had a big idea, but he had to sweat and suffer and sacrifice in order to make it work. *B.C Forbes*

To get your ideas across, use small word, big ideas and short sentence. *John Henry Patterson*

The best way to have a good idea is to have lots of ideas. *Linus Pauling*

For good ideas and true innovation, you need human interaction, conflict, argument, debate. *Margaret Hefferman*

If I have a thousand ideas and only one turns out to be good, I am satisfied. *Alfred Nobel*

Idea generation is first step, idea deployment is second. The first starts a process, the second delivers the profits. *Obinna Oleribe*

SECTION 2: ENTREPRENEURSHIP

Chapter 8: ENTREPRENEURSHIP: The IP4 OF ENTREPRENEURSHIP

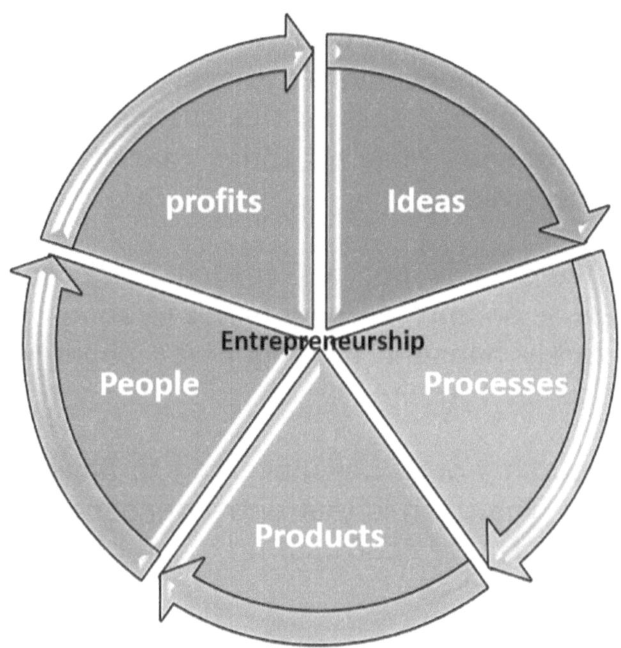

Entrepreneurship usually begins from IDEAS. Good and profitable ideas are processed into PRODUCTS. Finished products are marketed to PEOPLE who may eitheruse, sell, store or even gift the products. Every acceptance of the products by the people and their willingness to pay for the products result in PROFITS. This is the genesis of entrepreneurship – turning an amorphous idea into a finished product that yields income and profits.

Becoming a Successful Entrepreneur

"There are two kinds of people in business: Those with 20 years' experience and those with one year experience repeated 20 times."-Gene Dalton, BYU.

Life is not about what you want out of it, but how you get there. It's not the available resources you have in your possession that is important but knowing how well to use it and recycle it – thus the need for an entrepreneur.

An Entrepreneur is one who recognizes opportunities, creatively and/or innovatively gathers resources to exploit these opportunities, desires the chance to gain from these opportunities while accepting reasonable levels of risk and uncertainty.

Entrepreneurship is not a Get-Rich-Quick myth. The truth is life as an entrepreneur is not all about money as success rarely happens overnight. It's about what you want to do with your life.

Entrepreneurship does not make you to have free time all the time. The truth is that entrepreneurs work many long hours, but have control of time and can be involved in a variety of tasks.

Entrepreneurship does not make life easier. Another truth is that it gets more challenging because you must work harder, faster, smarter and longer; and must enjoy the journey.

Entrepreneurs are risk takers, and good entrepreneurs take only calculated risks.

And, entrepreneurs do not need to have great ideas to start. No. The truth is only good, doable, wanted or needed and rightly priced ideas sell.

To remain relevant and make all round progress, an entrepreneur must employ innovative ways of doing businesses rather than rely on some myths/tradition(s). Nothing good happens by accident. Though evil and failure may just happen, success is not a chance occurrence. The world is built upon random motion and to avoid randomization of destiny, deliberate efforts must be invested. In entrepreneurship, there is nothing like luck! Luck in entrepreneurship means **Labouring Under Clear Knowledge**.

Success does not happen by chance. While some work few hours to survive, others work all day to live. It is the extra steps that take you one step further, the extra effort that crowns your overall effort with great success and the extra investment that commands overflowing returns. Extra in ordinary makes ordinary *Extraordinary*!

Exceptional commitment is what breeds exceptional results, exceptional planning promotes exceptional performance. Only those with exceptional mentality manage great enterprises.

The Entrepreneurial Process:

An entrepreneur controls implementation by planning activities, preparing a program for their implementation, controlling their execution, having error prevention rather than error corrective mentality, ensuring operational research as implementation progresses, and regularly feeding back lessons learnt into the program.

Creativity and innovation must be supported and actively stimulated, new methods of doing things should be sought. Value adding activities must be identified and experimented on. Key word in entrepreneurship is: Do it another way ALWAYS.

Learning keeps you ahead. As an entrepreneur, you LEARN, LISTEN AND LEARN. It is your willingness to learn that makes you a leader in life. It takes learning to lead. Therefore, learn to do it right. Learn to do it better – then best, learn to please your clients, sponsors, and learn to be the best in the field.

You need to learn to use minimal resources to produce maximum output, outcomes and impacts. Seek to invest less and reap much, explore cost benefit analysis, maximize economy of scales, ensure you enjoy comparative advantages, stay within your core competencies, and become a specialist in an area. School yourself.

Paradoxically speaking, many profit-oriented organizations are managed at loss level, many businesses built with thousands of dollars end up liquidating over a period of few months to years – sometimes without breaking even and many so-called successful businessmen are living upon piles of debt.

The main difference is while some look at the short-term gains, others look at delayed gratification; while some are looking for ad-hoc measures, others are thinking and planning strategically; and while others just want to make it, others are programming for success.

It is your investment of today that determines your ultimate destination tomorrow. Invest in yourself today. To be successful as an entrepreneur;

1. Do what you enjoy

2. Take what you do seriously

3. Plan everything

4. Manage money wisely

5. Become a shameless promoter of self (without being obnoxious)

6. Build a top-notch business team

7. Invest in yourself

8. Develop the art of negotiation

9. Get and stay organized

Remember that there are two kinds of people in the world today – entrepreneurs and others. Choose one.

Chapter 9: STARTING WELL AND MAKING PROFITS AS AN ENTREPRENEUR

There are two kinds of people on the earth – entrepreneurs and those who work for them. Many people love entrepreneurship and several more want to become entrepreneurs, but few succeed as only one in every 20 start-ups survive to their fifth year. Although this statistics is abysmal, it may take a long time before this statistics will be changed.

Recently, I joined the marketing world to ensure that a product I came across which can change lives (health and wealth-wise) is placed in every home that needs it. This unique breakthrough product produces amazing results, adds value to living, ensures that ageing and death are delayed, and empowers people financially through their involvement and participation. Joining this product's marketing team opened me to what I choose to call the Eleven (11) Disciples of Failure as entrepreneurs.

1. **Excitement without Passion:** People listen to a marketer or product promoter and get excited. The product and business strategies are good. Immediately, they indicate their interest to use and/or market the product. They want to be part of this new business. They join out of excitement, but if they lack passion, they give up at the very first hurdle – believing that it cannot work. This

is, however, far from the truth. In the scriptures, these are seeds that fell by the way side in the parable of the sower!

2. **Passion without Knowledge:** Passion is good, but not enough. Every passionate individual without the right and adequate knowledge ends up sweating without good results. Be excited, be passionate, but please get knowledge. It takes knowledge to build great businesses. Get knowledge of the business, the product and the process. Get knowledge of the people, the customers, the manufacturers, and the business environment. Seek out knowledge from people, mentors, internet and associates. ***Go for knowledge***. That a man/woman stays without knowledge is NOT good!

3. **Passion without Skills:** Many are excited, and very passionate; and may enter the business with their all – big dreams, passion and resources. However, because they lack skills, they are unable to make the differences they desire. Challenges, obstacles and refusal from people demotivate them. Once demotivated, they lose the fire and begin to make excuses for their failures in all ramifications. *Please understand that passion alone cannot build sustainable businesses.*

4. **Wrong skills for Right Task:** Some people enter with the wrong set of skills. Some believe that their success in other businesses, career paths and even similar products will suffice. However, they forget that the only constant thing in life is change. Some apply skills that failed them in previous projects and products but are quick to excuse themselves and apply the same skills in their new ventures.

When they fail, instead of blaming their lack of skill or use of wrong skills, they blame the market, the system, or the product.

5. **Skills without strategies:** Functional skills are applied using tailored strategies. Every business has defined strategies that make implementation profitable. Use the tools, the videos, and every other material that have been tested and found acceptable and result yielding over the years. Working to develop new sets of strategies is good, but do not reinvent the wheel. Start with what is already available.

6. **Believing in wrong strategies:** Sustainable success in business requires identification and application of the right set of strategies. However, young and fresh entrepreneurs try many "fix-it" techniques to get rich quick. They prefer short cuts and fast track techniques and may not like to apply tested and proven strategies towards the growth of their businesses. Although these fast track and short-cuts will deliver immediate gains, these gains are temporary and very ephemeral. They never last and with time become rate limiting steps towards their growth and sustainable progress.

7. **Strategies without Plans:** Strategies must be translated into plans with goals, objectives, timelines, resource allocations, and appropriate definition of who, when, where, how, what and at what cost. Not developing and approving a functional plan results in wasted efforts and unproductive work. Plans prevent conflicts and allows for proper monitoring and evaluation of the project outputs and outcomes. It also allows for comparison

between planned and actuals. Plans ensure that resources are effectively and efficiently utilized by all key players in the business environment.

8. **Unfounded believes about entrepreneurship:** There are several people who believe that entrepreneurship is easy and a cheap way to make money. Others believe that becoming an entrepreneur gives them the freedom to do what they like. For instance, some believe that since they are in charge, they can go to work any time they want, work at their own space and pace, do what they like, and reap profit irrespective of their work culture and ethics. This is far from the truth as entrepreneurship is a serious business, played in a very complex and challenging environment where there are no real guidelines except your intuition and guts. Taking it lightly destroys the business and turns dreams into nightmares.

9. **Delegate and Disappear:** People starting new businesses wrongly believe that others will run their businesses for them. They either employ staff and hand over the business to them, or in multilevel marketing world, believe that their up-lines (or sponsors) will help them run their businesses. Some deliberately refuse to learn the required skills to manage their businesses, advance their vision and make money from them- this is a myth. The truth is that everybody runs their own businesses. Everyone has his/her own plans and will do anything to ensure that these plans succeed.

10. **Unwillingness to learn, unlearn and relearn:** Some people are unwilling to pay the price to learn how to run their businesses. Those who have some

experience are unwilling to learn new skills and unlearn the old failed ones. And those who have managed to succeed in some way, are unwilling to learn better ways of managing their business. All these make failure in business inevitable.

11. **Plans without Dedication and Discipline:** It takes dedication, devotion and discipline to effectively implement your plans. Plans unimplemented are wasted efforts. Entrepreneurship requires that the entrepreneur remains humble and meek – ready to learn; exercise discipline – ready to apply what was learned; and commits to the success of the business by being dedicated and diligent – which guarantees excellent outcomes and profitability.

Let me summarize the above 11 disciples of failure in these 12 basic facts of entrepreneurship

1. Excitement is NEVER enough; passion is critical to success in entrepreneurship.

2. Without appropriate knowledge and skills, entry into entrepreneurship ends faster than a 100-meter race.

3. Entrepreneurship is a path to financial independence and freedom, but making money from it is neither cheap nor easy

4. Working with strategies that failed in organized sectors will lead to further frustrations in entrepreneurship

5. Believing that others will do your work for you and deliver your success is the best example of self-deceit and foolishness

6. Taking no for an answer before exploring all relevant options is failure before you start – especially in multilevel marketing

7. Marketing your product to the wrong people is the easiest way of getting discouraged early in your business

8. Working and marketing with wrong strategies hinder progress and profits

9. Not believing in your ability to breakthrough, sell your product, and make profit in your business is an avoidable baggage.

10. Refusing to go for meetings, acquire new skills, strategies and knowledge and attend relevant programs is signature for complete failure

11. Not maximizing your God given talents, skills and other resources works against your career growth and progress in entrepreneurship, and

12. Running from, instead of towards opportunities – presentations, public events, new and relevant opportunities, trainings, etc. – is running from possible access to greatness.

I hope these simple nuggets will help make your forage into entrepreneurship a great success. I look forward to seeing you succeed beyond measures as an entrepreneur.

Chapter 10: STARTING A BUSINESS: TRUTHS AND MYTHS

Wikipedia defines a business (also known as an enterprise, a company or a firm) as "an organizational entity and legal entity made up of an association of people, be they natural, legal, or a mixture of both who share a common purpose and unite in order to focus their various talents and organize their collectively available skills or resources to achieve specific declared goals and are involved in the provision of goods and services to consumers."[1] This definition believes that businesses must involve more than one person who share common purpose and unite to achieve an objective. Although this may be true in some cases, it is not the truth in others as one person can start a business, manage it, and may then grow it to include others as the business expands.

This is why I also like the definition of BusinessDictionary. com which defined a business as "an organization or economic system where goods and services are exchanged for one another or for money."[2] According to BusinessDictionary.com, "Every business requires some form of investment and enough customers to whom its output can be sold on a consistent basis in order to make profit; and businesses can be privately owned, not-for-profit or state-owned."

---

[1]   https://en.wikipedia.org/wiki/Business

[2]   http://www.businessdictionary.com/definition/business.html

What are the myths about business ownership and management?

Myth 1: On Money: *Money is critical to starting a business:* Money will be needed, but money is NOT the first thing. Businesses begin with an idea, a concept or a strategy to solve a problem, meet a need, or create a new product. In majority of cases, the idea also generates the funds to start. I have heard many people say that they cannot work or start business because they do not have money. This is not only a lie, but the worse form of self-deceit. Most serious-minded people will start with what they have – their savings, resell of their personal belonging, their homes, etc. Keeping money where it belongs will empower many to start today.

Myth 2: On Start-Up: *A lot of money is needed to begin a business:* Start-up companies do NOT need a lot of money to start. Remember, if you jump up, you will fall. If you start with a lot of money, you might run into crisis as you do not have the capacity to manage that level of resources. This is why you must start small, grow and expand until you fill the room. One can start a future billion-dollar business with just 100 dollars. Ask Bill Gates! Therefore, waiting for when you have a large pool of resource to start a business may result in unnecessary delays and sometimes complete loss of the vision. It is important to understand this fact and begin from where you are per time.

Myth 3: On Passion: *Once I have passion, I can succeed in business:* Passion for a work, task, or vision is good; but this is not enough. I have heard many tell me how passionate they are about their dreams and vision. However, running with passion alone will always lead to crisis. Beyond passion, you need skills, knowledge and capacity. Passion delivers the intent; skills, capacity and knowledge deliver the results. Many very passionate persons have failed in their businesses and more will fail, until they get the required knowledge, skills and capacity to deliver on their assignments. While building your business, get necessary skills. Let your passion drive you towards getting the required skills and capacity to build a sustainable profitable business of your dreams.

Myth 4: On Success: *Money is what I need to succeed in business:* Money is necessary, but does not guarantee success. To succeed in business, there must be appropriate leadership of the organization. This must be exemplary. A successful leader must be good at leading himself (avoiding wastages), people, resources and time. Beyond leadership, every business must have the right kind of staff. One wrong person in the system can destroy the entire company. To succeed, there must be standards, policies and documented strategies. Having these in your head is not enough. They must be documented for all to see and use. Successful businesses are goal driven. These goals are SMART – simple, measurable, attainable, realistic/relevant and time bound. Thus, although money is important; exemplary leadership, right people, documented policies and strategies, and SMART goals are needed to make businesses successful.

Myth 5: On Space: *I need an office to manage my business:* Office is good, but not needed for all kinds of businesses. Some people start their businesses in their bedrooms and carry their phones or laptops to run them from any and every location they are. Wasting money to pay for an office when you do not need one is one fundamental error many start-ups make that results in their failure. Imagine using the little resources you have to pay for an office when you have little or no inflows.

This is a recipe for disaster. I have seen people change their office address frequently due to office cost and every time this happens, they lose customers. Some also stretch themselves to pay for spaces in the high-brow areas of the city. Begin where you are, and grow into large mega organizations.

Myth 6: On Time: *I can come to work anytime I like:* This is a very wrong mentality as time is both money and success. Being your own boss does not mean wasting your time as a resource. Running your own business requires that you spend more time on the business. Successful business owners see their business as their lives and have no clock in or clock out time. They manage their lives within the available time and ensure that every team member understands the value of time and invest the same towards the growth of their businesses. They are, therefore, exemplary time managers and investors.

However, there are basic truths about business. These include

Truth 1: On Success: *Successful businesses are worked out, they don't just happen.* This is as constant as the sun, moon and stars. Everything that is working is being worked out by someone. You must work out your vision to succeed. Nobody can work out your vision better than you. Diligence is the identity of successful business owners. Do you want to succeed in business? Then you must work it out. However, beyond just working (or hard work), you must work smart. Smart works result in better results. Smart works demand proper use of the brain to develop functional and efficient strategies, implementation and monitoring processes to ensure that results are in tandem with the inputs. Work hard but strive to work smart.

Truth 2: On Planning: *Proper preparation prevents poor performance.* It takes preparation to achieve remarkable results. Planning is the foundation for every great adventure. Like houses, you must plan to build a good business. There should be adequate time spent on planning the business. This may be used to develop the relevant policies, standards of practice, guidelines and manuals, depending on the type of business you wish to start. Time should also be spent in learning how to manage resources including people. Market analysis, segmentation and business plans should also be developed. Finally, it is important that early in the development of the business core values, mission, vision and purpose are established. Although these may change, it is important that the foundation be laid early in the development of the business. So, plan as failure to plan is planning to fail.

Truth 3: On People: *People are the life wire of businesses as internal and external customers make businesses succeed or fail.* No matter how small or big a business is, it needs people. These may be as staff, suppliers, customers, users, clients or even as marketers. It takes people to make profit in business. Business success is, therefore, people linked. Managing internal and external customers is critical and requires special skills. Although people are so crucial to business success, they are also the most difficult to manage – thus the need to learn people's skills including communication, negotiation, conflict management, marketing and emotional intelligence. Internal and external customers come with their various baggages. To succeed, you will have to learn how to manage these baggages towards organizational growth and development. Employment of staff must go through a defined process as you must ensure that the right people are employed to deliver the results you want. Understanding the need to have square pegs in square holes and ensuring that this is achieved is critical to the success of the business. Also, the welfare of the internal customers, their happiness and motivation affect how they respond to the external customers. So, do all you can to keep your staff motivated, happy and engaged. This is why their wages/salaries should be paid as and when due, their benefits delivered on time, and staff engagement enhanced through creative events like staff retreat, staff week of change and staff team trainings. Good business persons ensure that their staffers are always fully engaged and that external customers are well treated to ensure sustainability and healthiness of the organization.

Truth 4: On Purpose: *Businesses must meet basic or luxury needs of man to be sustainable.* There are four basic needs of man – food, shelter, health and clothing. There are also social needs such as education; and luxury needs/wants. Every successful business must meet one or more of these needs. Businesses that focus on basic needs always have customers irrespective of the economic climate of the nation. Therefore, decide on what needs to meet and align your business to meet them. As there is power in number, the bigger the market share targeted, the more the potential for market explosion. So, aim high – aim for larger markets like the telecommunication, Internet, cell phones, etc. Your business must focus on one or more of these global needs to remain relevant.

Truth 5: On Innovation and Continuous Improvement: *Today's success is tomorrow's failure.* Learn to continuously reinvent your business as the world is changing at the speed of light. Develop better processes, better strategies, and better products. Work to meet the needs of your customers long before they even recognize them. Be proactive, be future oriented, be visionary.

Many companies have liquidated because they failed to reinvent themselves – Kodak, Nokia, IBM, etc. Do not be like them. Change with time progressively. Many organizations have lost significant market share because they were too slow in accepting new trends – Swiss watch. Run with the world.

Now that you know the myths and the truths, debunk the myths and run with the truth and build a healthy, wealthy, and sustainable business.

Chapter 11: THE ROLLER COASTER OF BUSINESS DEVELOPMENT

Business results in financial independence. Business helps an individual achieve personal career goals. Business transforms individuals, communities, and societies resulting in changes that nothing else can deliver. Imagine the world without Microsoft, Intel, Apple, Boeing, and many others. Imagine the world without car manufacturers, GSM companies, Internet providers, Amazon, etc. Yes, imagine the world without banks, insurance companies, supermarkets, and various service organizations. The world rides and grows on businesses.

Every successful business was once an idea in somebody's mind. Every conglomerate you see today grew on the shoulders of men and women who believed in the business. Today, there are business initiators and business owners. There are also workers in various industries, companies, and establishments; that all benefit from the dreams and visions of founders and initiators. In life, you can work for the government, conglomerates, individuals or self. The choice is yours.

Every successful business goes through the roller coaster of maturity before they become a global brand. If you choose to manage your own business, for your business to succeed, you must understand the following and be willing to wait/work it out.

In this presentation, I will give four separate analogies to explain this roller coaster of business development.

First, businesses are like relationships. Every relationship sometimes begins by chance but grows by choice. We meet people by chance but become friends by choice. Although we cannot always determine who we meet, we can always determine who becomes our friend. Similarly, we come across business opportunities or ideas by chance – somebody tells us about it, we read about it in mails or on the internet, we hear about it in the news, seminars or conferences, or we stumble on people talking about the business – but we choose to either be part of it or let it go. Please understand that we are the choices we make and opportunities are maximized or lost through our choices, not by chance.

Secondly, businesses are like teams. Every team goes through five main stages of team development – forming, storming, norming, performing and adjourning/ transformation. In teams, we meet and get to know each other (forming); we fight for positions, prominence, and relevance (storming); we gradually begin to know our strengths and weaknesses and occupy our rightful positions (norming); then everyone begins to produce results, and we make profits from the union (performing); and when the entire work is done, we either dissolve the team (adjourning) or choose another problem to solve (transformation).

Similarly, businesses go through the same five stages. It begins with an idea, a problem, suggestion or an opportunity. Once you decide to join or start the business, you develop the required skills, make the required investments, and join or assemble the required team (forming); then you sail the ship as you are building it, trying to work the business even though you have limited skills and knowledge about the business and thus make your mistakes, lose money, annoy friends, and even fail a number of times (storming); then you learn from your mistakes, disengage none performing staff, change strategies, acquire better skills, institutionalize policies and guidelines and see a more stable business with minimal surprises and challenges (norming); then using all knowledge and skills acquired in the previous stages, you begin to produce better results and make profit with sustainable growth (performing); and with time you either start another arm of the business, or entirely different businesses (adjourning or transformation). Every business goes through these fundamental five stages.

Thirdly, businesses are like trees. If you want immediate, short-term profit (say within a year), plant maize or corn. If you want a profit within two to three years, plant pumpkin, tomato, or cassava. If you want a five to ten-year profit, plant bamboo or apple. But if you want a long-term, lasting profit, plant an iroko tree, orange, mango and palm tree.

So is a business. The amount of time and kind of seed (idea) you pursue determines how quickly you can make a profit and for how long you will make a profit. People get so easily discouraged when they are not making a profit immediately. But people go to nursery, primary, secondary and universities to acquire certificates they use to look for jobs, and when they get these jobs, they can work for life in the same organization. They begin to make a profit from their certificates after over 16 to 20 years investment in their education. No wonder, the rewards are the same for life. Similarly, if you want life time rewards from your business, invest in it for a long time – maybe for some years and sit back to enjoy the benefits of the business.

Finally, businesses are like children. They are born, grow, marry and have their own children. These do not happen in one day. Before they are born, they stay in the womb for about nine months. If delivered early, they are called ***premature***. Allow your business to mature in your mind, and/or current state before moving to the next phase. During the growth phase, children fall and rise again, take risks, make mistakes, learn and relearn, and they build relationships and strength. Similarly, in running a new business, understand that you will fail, take a risk, build new relationships, learn/unlearn/relearn, and build stamina to overcome challenges. As you build your business, learn and allow yourself to marry (buy into other businesses, partner with other people, and if possible, merge your business with somebody else's business). This allows for accelerated growth and access to new territories and frontiers you may not have known. And like children, at the right age, have your children – diversify, develop branches, open new offices, grow into new markets and do other things.

All global conglomerates today began small. Do not be afraid to start small. All global conglomerates began with just an idea. Put your idea to work. All big businesses today had their days of challenges and problems. Do not be afraid of challenges and storms – face them. All major business owners took risks – the bigger the risk, the greater the benefits. Take calculated risks.

A Chinese proverb says that the best time to plant a tree was twenty years ago, the second best time is now. Today, is a new opportunity to start. This may be your first outing into the business world, or you started before and failed. Start all over again. Behind every successful man, there is a story of a test, challenges, and problems encountered, faced and resolved. Be a victor. Face your mountains and turn your obstacles into stepping stones. It is time to do that thing you have long waited for. It is time to put wheels on your dreams and visions.

What, therefore, is this roller coaster of business development? You start, do well for a while, fail, stand up again, learn, restart, run, fall, stand and continue, make profits, make friends and become a global brand. As there is no walking without falling, so is there no successful business without challenges. Rise thee up, and face them now.

Now is your time.

Chapter 12: RUNNING SUCCESSFUL ORGANIZATIONS

It is said that success has many friends; but failure is an orphan. Even though success is relative and has no clearly defined metric by which it can be measured, it can be said to mean achieving all an individual or a group has set to achieve. However, true success is progressive and thus progressively gets better, moves the person or organization progressively forward with greater milestones and achievements as the days and years go by.

Every organization or company is set up with a **Big Overarching Goal** - to be successful. However, studies have shown that of all organizations set up within a year, barely 50% make it pass the first year and even fewer survive the second year. This has been blamed on many factors including unfavourable business climate.

I want to state that businesses or organizations do not fail, people do. Therefore, why we have so many failed organizations is that many businesses and organizational leaders are not equipped with the prerequisite knowledge and skills required to run successful organizations. Furthermore, they are ignorant of what type of organizational structure to adopt, management of group dynamics, and the characteristics of successful organizations.

An organization is a social unit of people that is structured and managed to satisfy a need or pursue a collective goal. Various organizational structures exist of which 3 are most prominent: Functional, matrix and projectized.

A functional organizational structure is one in which individuals are grouped according to the specialized set of tasks they perform. In such structure, individuals within a functional division is well acquainted with what is attainable within his division, but lacks a good understanding of what is expected from other functional units and how they together achieve the organization's objectives. Here, things are done in an operational manner and the functional manager has little or no authority over budgets nor has the capacity to develop and execute good plans.

A matrix organizational structure is a blend of functional and product/projects structure (also known as projectized structure). It may be weak (more of a functional structure), balanced or strong (more of a projectized structure). The matrix structure uses teams of individuals from different functional units for the purpose of achieving a set of objectives. The advantage being the weakness of one member of the team is made up for by other members with other specialty.

A projectized organizational structure is a structure set up for the purpose of running businesses as projects. It is managed by a project manager who has a good understanding of time, quality and cost implications in project success, and is able to deliver the project within acceptable standards as defined in the project initiation documents.

Having understood this, it is important to state that an organization is a set of individuals working together and is affected by individual/group dynamics. Every organization has a life cycle which is characterized by various developmental stages which include: the forming, storming, norming, performing, and adjourning stages.

In the *forming* stage, members determine their place in the organization, go through a testing or orientation process, and are more independent. The organization in the *storming* stage has members who react negatively to the demands of whatever tasks need to be accomplished; conflicts arise as members resist influence, and there is a high level of emotion. In the *norming* stage, in-group feelings and cohesiveness develop, and members accept the rules of behaviour and discover new ways to work together. In the *performing* stage, the group becomes quite functional in dealing with tasks and responsibilities. Members have worked through issues of membership and roles; they focus their efforts and achieve their goals. In the *adjourning* stage, the group brings finality to the process, tasks are closed, and members anticipate a change in relationships.

Having looked at these pertinent issues with respect to business, it is time to take a look at what are the characteristics of a successful business.

Successful businesses share common characteristics that almost guarantee a certain level of achievement. These traits typically involve the people who run the organization, the business plans they follow, the efficiency level of their processes and how well they interact with their customer base.

Strategy: It is said that where there is no vision, there is no direction and a group of people is bound to fail. One very important trait successful businesses share is a strong vision, purpose and strategic direction, to which every member of the organization is committed to. This means having a statement of principles that is not just some high-sounding words tacked up on the wall of the company cafeteria, but a rather clear set of values that actually influence a company's operations and give employees a strong sense of pride in their organizations.

Cross-Functional: Most successful organizations are built around the Matrix or Projectized-type organization structure against the traditional functional lines. Organizations that survive in this modern era do not operate as separate silos but as a web of inter-related units working together with a clear knowledge of what is expected of their core areas, other units and how together this helps to achieve the organizational goals.

Clearly Defined Roles and Responsibility: A well-defined strategy helps an organization understand what capacity and capabilities is needed to achieve it. Successful organizations set up structures which define these responsibilities, relationships and ensure that they are maintained and reviewed at all time as business demands evolve.

Right People: For any organization to succeed it has to have the right people on board occupying the right positions. Every successful organization possesses systems and processes which is used to engage the right set of individuals. They do not just go for every capable individual but those with the capacity to share the organization's vision and commitment.

Culture & Values: An organization's success or failure is influenced by the kind of business environment created around it. The culture and values obtainable within an organization has the capacity to influence every new employee to be either most productive or unproductive. Every successful organization strives to ensure that the systems, symbols, and behaviours that leaders and other employees are exposed to within an organization must align to the desired culture to achieve the business strategy.

Customer Focused: An organization's success is determined by customers' satisfaction. If the persons for whom you are in business are not satisfied with your product or services, success will be far-fetched. As such, organizations which make it to the top strive to retain their customers, while gaining new ones. This is achieved through anticipating what customers want, satisfying it and surpassing their expectation. A truly satisfied customer is one of the indices for a highly successful organization.

The overlying characteristic of a successful organization is, therefore, its **leadership**. An organization is nothing without its leaders. For an organization to attain a high level of achievement, it must possess the right set of leaders at every stratum within the organizational structure. Processes, systems, and structures do not drive themselves but leaders do. It is the responsibility of the leader to conceive the vision, develop the strategies, plan the work and drive its accomplishment. An ideal leader would ensure that a structure which clearly defines the roles of accountability and relationships is established and maintained.

Leadership is a process by which a person influences others to accomplish an objective and directs the organization in a way that makes it more cohesive and coherent. It is a process of social influence in which one person can enlist the aid and support of others in the accomplishment of a common task.

Successful organizations have leaders instead of managers and supervisors. Leaders serve as inspiration to the team of employees. They are visionary and pathfinders. They do not just implement solutions, but they help to create them.

Most successful organizations understand that to remain competitive, they should nurture and groom leaders at every level of the organization, so they set up systems to ensure that every employee within the organization is trained and equipped to be a leader.

The right leader MUST, therefore, be measured on the **BE KNOW DO** paradigm.

BE – Is he a professional, loyal to the organisation, performs selfless service, takes personal responsibility; honest, competent, committed; full of integrity, courageous, straightforward, and imaginative?

KNOW – Does he know the four factors of leadership - follower, leader, communication, and situation? Does he know him/herself – strengths and weakness of his/her character, knowledge, and skills; human nature - human needs, emotions, and how people respond to stress; his/her job –daily, weekly, monthly and annual tasks and expectations; and the organisation- organizational climate and culture, official and unofficial leaders, clients and customers, relevant networks, etc.?

DO – Can he provide excellent direction - goal setting, problem solving, decision making, planning; implement - communicating, coordinating, supervising, evaluating;

motivate- develop moral and esprit in the organisation, train, coach, counsel; and get his hands dirty when the going gets tough? These are the BE KNOW DO of the ideal leader.

Chapter 13: STARTING AND MANAGING A PROFITABLE BUSINESS

The richest men in the world today are not employed by anybody, but employers of others. They are businessmen who have started and managed profitable businesses over the years. Top 10 of these in 2019 are

- Jeff Bezos: Net worth $112 billion
- Bill Gates: Net worth $90 billion
- Warren Buffett: Net worth $84 billion
- Bernard Arnault: Net worth $72 billion
- Mark Zuckerberg: Net worth $71 billion
- Amancio Ortega: Net worth $70 billion
- Carlos Slim Helu: Net worth $67.1 billion
- Charles & David Koch (tied): Net worth $60 billion
- Larry Ellison: Net worth $58.5 billion
- Michael Bloomberg: Net worth $50 billion

Everybody is busy, and may be said to be in business – but not all are in profitable businesses. Only profitable business, drawn from profitable ideas can pay bills, and give one the life he or she wants.

Many people are not in business because they are paid monthly of forth-nightly salaries. Others enjoy daily pay from blue collar jobs. But salaries/daily pays are bribes that deny you your inheritance in life by suspending your passion and dreams while you run that of others.

To start a business, six things are very vital;

- Big dreams – You must have a big hairy audacious dream. If you can dream it, you can make it happen.
- Great Ideas – This must be fully processed, reviewed and ready for implementation. Having an idea is not good enough – it must be processed and ready for use.
- Passion – Passion is the engine that drives dreams and ideas into reality. You must have an amazing passion for success that will transform your ideas and dreams into expressions of reality with profits and income that are both sustainable and life changing.
- Skills – Passion is never enough in business management. Skills are critical. You must develop the capacity and competence – that is skills – to effectively implement the processes that will deliver your dreams and ideas. School yourself. Get skills. Be trained to be trusted.
- Resources - internal and external – These are the oil that fuel the engine of business success. These include financial, human, material and machines. The amount of resources needed varies from business to business. But no business can effectively take off without adequate relevant resources. One must, however, focus on necessities rather than luxuries.
- No quit mentality – As businesses have a roller coaster life cycle, you must have a no quit mentality to succeed. Challenges and obstacles should be seen as stepping stones and learning points. Every pain point should be transformed into a profit

point. A problem solving mentality is highly needed towards a successful implementation of ideas and pursuit of dreams.

To succeed with a no quit mentality, you must have or develop the following;

- Desire to destroy your comfort zone and succeed in this uncharted zone of business management
- Decide to either succeed or succeed irrespective of the challenges.
- Dedicate your time and energy to building a sustainable and life changing business in an area of your choice.
- Diligently seek opportunities within and outside your warm networks.
- Give yourself completely to it despite what others are saying or not saying, and
- Focus on your goals, targets and deliverables at all times. It is important you develop your Key Success Factors and make sure that they are timed and achieved.

Successful businesses solve human problems. These may be in the area of health, education, nutrition, poverty, shelter, clothing, spiritual, etc. Therefore find what you can do to solve any of these human problems and the more you solve, the more money you make.

Strategies: To solve these problems you can engage in buying and selling of commodities, provision of services, manufacturing of goods, or networks/connectivity management.

Benefits: Businesses have amazing benefits which may include (but not limited to) daily, weekly and monthly pay; freedom; choice and options; legacy; empowerment of others; creativity and innovation; better income and Better life; etc.

You can own your own business by beginning from where you are right now. What you have is enough to start if you have an idea, or a dream worth pursuing. You can also lookout for divine opportunities in your area of interest and passion.

In making a choice, be careful what system you buy into as system can either limit or advance you.

Once you start, go for more skills. This can be physical or virtual. Find a mentor to help reduce your learning curve. And when the need arises, call for help.

Now start.

Dr Obinna O Oleribe is a project management, leadership and public health consultant. He has five fellowships including FRCP and FWACP, a doctorate degree in public health, three master's degrees, and two bachelor's degrees. He is a multiple award (academic and non-academic) winner. He currently works as a Chief Executive Officer of Excellence and Friends Management Care Center (EFMC) Abuja as well as oversees several other business interests including Modern Health Hospital, Centre for Family Health Initiative, and Excellence and Friends Management Consult. He serves as the West African Consultant to BroadReach Consulting LLC. A trainer, public speaker, life coach, and mentor; he is married with wonderful children.

www.ingramcontent.com/pod-product-compliance
Lightning Source LLC
Chambersburg PA
CBHW031139250726
48655CB00002B/742